Three Great Plays of Shakespeare

Level 4

Retold by Karen Holmes
Series Editors: Andy Hopkins and Jocelyn Potter

Pearson Education Limited
Edinburgh Gate, Harlow,
Essex CM20 2JE, England
and Associated Companies throughout the world.

ISBN 0 582 426863

This edition first published 2000

5 7 9 10 8 6

Typeset by Pantek Arts Ltd, Maidstone, Kent
Set in 11/14pt Bembo
Printed in China
SWTC/05

Published by Pearson Education Limited in association with
Penguin Books Ltd, both companies being subsidiaries of Pearson Plc

Acknowledgements:
Photographs © BBC Worldwide

For a complete list of titles available in the Penguin Readers series, please write to your local
Pearson Education office or to: Penguin Readers Marketing Department,
Pearson Education, Edinburgh Gate, Harlow, Essex CM20 2JE.

Contents

Introduction

'And so,' the prince said, *'this dark and cloudy morning has brought a sad peace. There will never be a sadder story than the story of Romeo and Juliet.'*

Romeo and Juliet tells the story of two important families in Verona, in Italy. The families hate each other. Romeo, the son of Lord Montague, falls in love with Juliet, the daughter of Lord Capulet. But when people hate each other, everybody around them is affected. The story does not end happily because Romeo and Juliet cannot escape from the war between their families and live happily together. In this play, hate has more power over people's lives than love.

All three stories in this book have sad endings. In each story, the main characters die. They die because they, or others, are weak, greedy or very foolish.

Lord and Lady Macbeth (*Macbeth*) are greedy, and as a result a lot of people die. Macbeth is also weak. Lady Macbeth says, 'Macbeth is too kind, too gentle. There are things that he must do but he is afraid to do them. I must speak to him, and make him brave.' He becomes a murderer and a cruel king because his wife tells him that he must perform evil acts. By the end of the play, Macbeth does not care about anybody. When his wife dies, he says, 'It would be better if she died at another time.'

In the third story, *King Lear*, the king is an a very old man. His great age makes him weak and foolish. He does not understand the characters of his three daughters, and he believes Goneril and Regan when they say that they love him. He thinks that his youngest daughter, Cordelia, does not love him because she refuses to use such fine words. But Goneril and Regan are greedy for power and they do not care about their father.

Many of the characters in these stories have a lot of faults but, like real people, they have good qualities and moments of greatness too. Macbeth is a fine army commander. He wins an important war and King Duncan admires him. Lear is a great king. The King of France thinks that he is a good man, and the Earl of Gloucester loves him. Even the Montagues and the Capulets end their quarrel – but too late.

William Shakespeare is the most famous writer of plays in the English language. He was born in Stratford-upon-Avon in 1564, six years after Elizabeth I became Queen of England. He wrote thirty-nine plays; thirty-four of these are still regularly seen on the stage. Many are famous as films too. He also wrote hundreds of poems.

We do not know very much about William Shakespeare's life. We think that he went to school in Stratford. He married Anne Hathaway in 1582, and they had three children: Suzanna (born in 1583), Hamnet and Judith (born together in 1585).

After that, we know nothing about his life until 1592. He went to London, where he began to write successful plays. He became an important member of a theatre company, which performed at two London theatres: the Globe and the Blackfriars. His plays were given special performances at the courts of Queen Elizabeth I and King James I. Shakespeare's success made him a wealthy man, and in 1597 he bought New Place, the largest house in Stratford. We believe that he left London and went back to live at New Place in 1610. He continued to write plays until he died in Stratford in 1616.

We know more about Shakespeare's plays than we know about the writer. For 400 years, people have studied every word that Shakespeare wrote. He wrote amusing plays with happy endings, like *A Midsummer Night's Dream* and *Twelfth Night*. He also wrote historical plays; nine of these are about English kings. The third type were sad and serious plays, like the three stories in this book.

Romeo and Juliet

This is the story of the love of Romeo and Juliet. Romeo was the son of Lord Montague, the head of the Montague family. Juliet was the daughter of Lord Capulet.

The Montagues and the Capulets were two important families in the city of Verona who had had a terrible quarrel. Even their servants hated each other, and they fought and cursed each other whenever they met.

One day, two servants from the house of Capulet saw two servants from the house of Montague and they began to fight. Benvolio, a friend of Romeo, saw the fight. He liked peace and quiet, so he hated to see people fighting.

'Stop!' he cried, but it was already too late. Tybalt, a young and angry Capulet, had arrived in the street.

'Help me to stop this fight,' Benvolio cried to him.

Tybalt pulled out his sword. 'I hate all Montagues and I hate you!' he cried, and he began to fight Benvolio.

The noise and the shouting brought officers of the law to the scene of the fight. Then Lord Capulet and his wife arrived, and Lord Montague and his wife. The heads of the two families pulled out their swords.

Suddenly Prince Escalus, the Prince of Verona, appeared.

'You men, you are like wild animals!' he said to them angrily. 'Your quarrels spoil the quiet of our streets. Listen to me! If you make trouble in the streets of Verona again, you will pay for it with your lives! Now, everyone must leave this place.'

Lord and Lady Montague and Benvolio left last.

'Where is Romeo?' asked Lady Montague. 'I am very glad that he did not take part in this fight.'

'Very early this morning,' Benvolio said, 'I could not sleep. I walked out into the woods on the west of the city, and I saw Romeo there, alone. I went towards him, but when he saw me, he hid among the trees. I decided not to follow him.'

Romeo's father, Lord Montague, said, 'Many people have seen Romeo early in the morning, weeping alone. When the sun comes up, he goes into his room and he shuts out the daylight. I am afraid for him.'

'Do you know why he is unhappy?' Benvolio asked.

'He will not tell me,' Lord Montague replied.

'Look! Here he comes,' said Benvolio. 'Go home. I will try to find out why he is unhappy.'

He quickly learned the reason for Romeo's sadness.

'I love the beautiful Rosaline, but she does not love me,' Romeo said.

Benvolio tried to help his good friend. 'Forget her. Don't think about her,' he said.

'How can I forget her?' Romeo asked.

'Look around you. Look at other beautiful women.'

'When I look at other women, I see that Rosaline is the most beautiful of all!'

In another street in Verona, Count Paris was talking to Lord Capulet, Juliet's father. Paris was the prince's nephew.

'I would like to marry Juliet. What do you say?' Paris asked.

'She is my only child and she is too young,' said Capulet. 'Let two more summers pass before she marries. But you can speak to her and try to win her love. Every year at this time I give a great feast. It will take place tonight. All my friends will come to my house and dance. You must come too – then you can talk to Juliet.'

Capulet called a servant and said, 'On this piece of paper there is a list of names. Find these people and ask them to come to dinner at my house tonight.' Then he walked away with Paris.

'This is going to be quite difficult for me because I cannot read,' the servant thought.

Benvolio and Romeo came along the street. They were still talking about Romeo's unhappiness.

'Please, sir, can you read?' Capulet's servant asked. He gave Romeo the list of names.

Romeo read out the list for him: 'Martino and his wife and daughters; Anselm and his beautiful sisters; Mercutio and his brother Valentine; Lucio and Helena; Rosaline ... Where are these people going to meet?'

'At my master's house tonight,' the servant said.

'Who is your master?' Romeo asked.

'My master is the great and rich Lord Capulet. If you are not a Montague, come and drink wine with us all.'

'This is the chance I wanted for you!' said Benvolio happily. 'Go there. Compare your Rosaline with other women. You will see that she is not more beautiful than them.'

'You are wrong,' Romeo replied. 'Since the world began, the sun has never seen a woman as beautiful as Rosaline. I will go to the Capulet's feast – but only to look at Rosaline.'

◆

Juliet was with her mother, Lady Capulet, and her nurse.

'You were a pretty little baby when I came here,' said the nurse. 'Now I have one wish. I want to live long enough to see you married!'

'I want to talk to you about marriage,' Lady Capulet said to her daughter. 'Juliet, do you want to find a husband?'

'I have not thought about it very much,' answered Juliet.

'Here in Verona, younger girls are already important ladies and mothers. I will tell you now that Count Paris hopes to win your love.'

'He is a fine man, almost a perfect man!' cried the nurse.'He is the finest man in Verona!'

'You will see him tonight at our feast,' Lady Capulet said.'He needs a wife, and you will make his life complete.'

◆

The evening came. Romeo and his friends, Mercutio and Benvolio, put on hats to hide their faces and went to the feast at the Capulets' house.

But Tybalt heard Romeo's voice.

'I know that voice!' he said.'That man is a Montague. What is he doing here?' He called to his servant,'Fetch my sword!'

'What is the matter?' asked Lord Capulet.

'That man is a Montague. He is our enemy!'

'Is it young Romeo?'

'Yes,' Tybalt said. ·

'Let him stay. The people of Verona say that he is a good young man, and he is behaving like a gentleman tonight. Don't look so angry. We must entertain our guests.'

Tybalt was very angry but he had to obey his uncle.

At that moment, something wonderful happened to Romeo; he saw a beautiful girl. She was lovely, sweet, happy and good. As he watched her, he forgot about Rosaline. Now he was truly, deeply in love.

He went to her and touched her hand.'Your hand is too soft for my rough touch,' he said.'But my lips are ready to touch your gentle hand with a kiss.' He kissed her hand.'You have lips, too,' he said.

Juliet found that she was in love with him, and so they kissed.

The nurse came to them.'Your mother wants to speak to you,' she said to Juliet.

'Who is her mother?' asked Romeo.

'Her mother is Lady Capulet,' the nurse replied.

'Oh, no!' Romeo thought. 'I have fallen in love with the daughter of my enemy!'

Everyone began to leave, and Romeo went with them. Juliet watched him go.

'Come here, nurse,' she said. 'Who is that gentleman over there? Go and ask his name.'

The nurse came back and said, 'His name is Romeo. He is a Montague, the only son of your great enemy.'

◆

Later that same night, Romeo's friends searched the streets of Verona for him.

Romeo was standing below Juliet's lighted window when he saw her there.

'It is Juliet!' he said quietly. 'Oh! It is my love! She is as beautiful as the sun in the sky. She is looking up at the stars, but her eyes are brighter than they are. The birds will see them and think that it is already daytime.'

Juliet looked out of her window and rested her face on her hand. She was thinking of Romeo. She did not know that he was there, listening.

'Oh, Romeo, Romeo, why is your name Romeo?' she said. 'Leave your family and change your name. If you cannot, I will leave the Capulets. It is only your name that is my enemy. But what is important about a name? If a rose had another name, it would still smell sweet. Change your name so we can be together.'

'Call me "Love",' Romeo called up to her. 'That will be my name. I will never be Romeo again. I hate my name because it is your enemy.'

'How did you get there?' Juliet asked. 'The walls are high.'

'Stone walls cannot keep out love,' Romeo said.

Juliet was afraid. 'If my family see you here, they will kill you,' she said.

'*Stone walls cannot keep out love,*' Romeo said.

'If their hatred ends my life,' said Romeo, 'then I will die. I do not care. I do not want to live without your love.'

'Do you love me? I know that you will say "yes". But tell me the truth.'

'Lady, I promise by the moon that touches the tops of those fruit trees with silver.'

'Oh! Don't promise by the moon,' Juliet said. 'The moon changes every month. I do not want your love to change like the moon.'

'What shall I promise by?' Romeo asked.

'Do not promise. You make me happy, but this love has come very suddenly. I must go now.'

'No! Wait!' Romeo cried.

At that moment the nurse called.

'I can hear a noise,' said Juliet. 'Sweet Romeo, stay here for a moment. I will come back.'

She went inside, but soon she returned.

'Dear Romeo,' she said, 'if you truly love me and wish to marry me, send a message tomorrow. I will send someone to collect your message. Tell me where and at what time you will marry me and my life will be yours. I will follow you, my lord, across the world.'

The nurse called again. Juliet went in and then came out again.

'Romeo!'

'My sweet?'

'At what time tomorrow shall I send someone to you?' she asked.

'At nine o'clock,' Romeo replied.

'My messenger will find you. It is almost morning, so I must let you go. Good night! Good night! I am sad to leave you, but it is a sweet sadness. I will not stop saying "Good night" until tomorrow.'

She went back into her room.

'Let sleep rest on your eyes,' said Romeo, 'and peace in your heart. I wish that I could rest in such a sweet place.' He turned away. 'I must go to Friar Lawrence and tell him about Juliet,' he said to himself. 'He will help me.'

◆

Friar Lawrence was a man of God. Romeo and Juliet both knew him. Early the next morning, he was picking plants outside his cell. He knew a lot about plants. He used them to make sick people better, or to help tired or ill people sleep.

When he saw Romeo running towards him, Friar Lawrence was very surprised.

'Why are you here so early?' asked the friar. 'Young men sleep late in the morning. Can't you sleep? Were you thinking of Rosaline?'

'No, I could not sleep, but I was not thinking about Rosaline. I have forgotten her name and all the unhappiness that went with it. I must tell you what happened. Last night I went to a feast at my enemy's house. There I fell in love with the beautiful daughter of Lord Capulet, and she loves me. We want you to marry us today.'

'Oh! What a change!' cried Friar Lawrence. 'Yesterday you loved Rosaline! Now you tell me that you love someone else. I do not like it. It is too sudden.'

'Don't be angry with me. Juliet loves me, and Rosaline does not. Please marry us today.'

'Rosaline knew that you were not really in love,' said the wise friar. 'So I will marry you. This marriage may turn the hatred between your two families into love.'

◆

Mercutio and Benvolio were searching for Romeo. Mercutio was a member of Prince Escalus's family, and one of Romeo's friends.

'Romeo was not at his father's house last night,' Benvolio said. 'Tybalt is looking for him. He is angry because Romeo went to the Capulets' feast, and he wants to fight him!'

Then Romeo arrived. He looked very happy.

'What has happened to you?' Mercutio asked him.

Before Romeo could answer, the nurse and her servant arrived.

'Go to my father's house,' Romeo said to Benvolio and Mercutio. 'I will follow you soon.'

He waited until they had gone, then he spoke to the nurse.

'Tell Juliet,' said Romeo, 'to go to Friar Lawrence this afternoon. He will marry us in his cell. My man, Balthazar, will meet you in one hour behind the church. He will bring you a ladder. Tonight I will climb up to Juliet's room.'

'Will Balthazar keep your secret?'

'Yes,' Romeo replied. 'He is a good servant.'

'Paris wants to marry my lady Juliet, but I know that you will make her happy,' the nurse said.

'Goodbye,' Romeo said. 'Give my dearest love to Juliet.'

'I will, a thousand times,' she promised.

Juliet was waiting for the nurse to return.

'Oh! Here she comes! Dearest nurse, are you bringing me news? Have you met him? What does he say about our marriage?'

'Can you visit Friar Lawrence today?' asked the nurse.

'Yes,' Juliet said.

'Then go to his cell. Romeo is waiting there to make you his wife. Ah, that has brought the blood to your face! Now I must go and fetch a ladder. Your Romeo will climb up into your room tonight.'

'Dear, good nurse!' Juliet said.

◆

That same afternoon, the friar married Romeo and Juliet.

'Heaven smiles upon this wedding,' Friar Lawrence said to

them. 'I hope that there will not be trouble later.'

'I do not care,' Romeo cried.

'Great and sudden love can bring great sadness,' the friar replied.

◆

A little later on the same day, Benvolio and Mercutio were talking together.

'Mercutio,' said Benvolio, 'let us go away. The Capulets are somewhere in these streets and I do not want to meet them. They will want to fight.'

He was right. Suddenly Tybalt and his friends came into the street. Tybalt and Mercutio started to quarrel. Then Romeo came along the street and Tybalt began to shout at him.

'You are my enemy!' Tybalt cried. 'Pull out your sword!'

'I do not want to be your enemy,' Romeo replied. 'I love the Capulet name as much as I love my own name.'

But Tybalt wanted to fight. 'Pull out your sword!' he shouted again to Romeo.

'I will not quarrel with you,' Romeo said.

Mercutio was surprised. He did not want Romeo to be friendly with Tybalt. 'I will fight you instead,' he shouted to Tybalt, and a fight began.

'Stop, gentlemen,' Romeo cried. 'The prince told us not to fight in these streets.'

He tried to stand between them, but Tybalt's sword went under Romeo's arm and wounded Mercutio. Tybalt ran away.

'I am wounded!' cried Mercutio. 'A curse on both your families! Fetch a doctor!'

'Be brave, man!' said Romeo. 'I hope it is not a bad wound.'

'It is not very deep, but it is bad enough. Look for me tomorrow, and you will have to find my tomb. Why did you stand between us? Tybalt's sword passed under your arm. Help me into a house, Benvolio.'

'I will fight you instead,' he shouted to Tybalt.

Soon afterwards, Benvolio returned. 'Oh, Romeo,' he said, 'brave Mercutio is dead.'

Everything seemed black for Romeo. His dear friend was dead and Tybalt hated him more than ever. The prince would punish them for quarrelling in the streets of Verona and for Mercutio's death.

Then Tybalt came back.

'Tybalt is alive, and my friend Mercutio is dead!' cried Romeo. 'Now I do not care what I do. One of us will die with Mercutio.'

There was a terrible fight between Romeo and Tybalt, and Tybalt fell dead.

'Escape, Romeo!' cried Benvolio. 'People are coming. The prince will be angry, and he will punish you with death.'

As the unhappy Romeo ran away, the prince, the Montagues and the Capulets arrived.

'Who started this quarrel?' asked the prince.

Lady Capulet stood weeping over the body of the dead Tybalt as Benvolio tried to explain.

'Romeo tried to stop the fight between Tybalt and Mercutio but he could not. Tybalt killed Mercutio, then Romeo killed Tybalt.'

Lady Capulet did not believe him. 'Benvolio belongs to the Montague family. He is lying. Romeo killed Tybalt and he must not live.'

'I will have to punish Romeo for Tybalt's death,' said the prince. 'He must leave the city and never return. If I find Romeo in Verona, he will die!'

◆

Juliet was waiting for the night.

'Come, gentle night!' she said. 'Bring me my Romeo and let me hold him in my arms. And when he dies, take him and cut him into little stars. He will make the face of heaven look very fine. Everyone will love the night. Ah, here comes my nurse. Have you brought the ladder?'

The nurse came in carrying a ladder.

'Why are you weeping?' Juliet asked.

'Tybalt is dead,' she said. 'Romeo killed him!'

'No!' Juliet cried. 'Don't say such a terrible thing.'

'It is true. I saw the wound on Tybalt's body. Romeo killed him and now he must leave the city. Oh, Tybalt! Tybalt was an honest gentleman!'

'Tybalt wanted to kill my husband. Now my husband is alive, and Tybalt is dead, but Romeo must leave Verona. These words mean death to me. I cannot live without him.'

'Go to your room,' said the nurse. 'I will find Romeo for you. I know where he is. He is in Friar Lawrence's cell.'

'Oh, find him! Give him this ring. Tell him to come and say his last goodbye to me!'

◆

At the same time, Friar Lawrence was trying to help Romeo.

'The Capulets want the prince to kill you,' the friar said. 'But he has only ordered you to leave Verona.'

'Never! Let me die instead,' Romeo cried.

'Stay calm. The world is great and wide.'

'There is no world for me except Verona. Juliet is here. Let me die if I cannot stay with her. Give me poison or a sharp knife. Let me die!'

'Don't say that. You are talking like a madman,' the friar said.

The nurse arrived. 'I have come from Lady Juliet,' she said. 'Where is Romeo?'

'He is here,' the friar replied. 'His tears are making him crazy.'

'Juliet is the same. She just weeps and weeps.'

'Tell me,' said Romeo. 'Does she think I am a murderer? Does she still love me?'

'She does not say anything. She calls out your name and then Tybalt's name,' the nurse said.

Romeo was very unhappy. He tried to drive his sharp dagger into his heart, but the friar stopped him.

'Stop! Are you a man?' Friar Lawrence asked. 'You cry like a woman. You behave wildly like an animal. I thought you were strong. If you kill yourself, you will kill your lady. She lives for you. Be strong, man! Go to Juliet and help her. Then, early tomorrow morning, you must leave Verona and go to Mantua. Stay there until the prince forgives you. Nurse, go to your lady. Tell her that Romeo is coming to her.'

'Yes,' said Romeo.

'Here, sir,' the nurse said. 'Juliet wants you to have this ring.'

'Go now,' the friar said to Romeo. 'Leave for Mantua tomorrow. I will send your servant there with messages for you.'

◆

That night, Romeo climbed up the ladder into Juliet's room. It was a strange night for the new husband and wife. They were wonderfully happy, but very frightened.

At the first light of day, Romeo had to leave.

'Must you go now?' said Juliet. 'It is still night.'

'Look, love!' said Romeo. 'The light is shining through the clouds in the east, and the stars are pale now. Daylight is waiting on the mountain tops. I must go now and live – or stay and die.'

Juliet was frightened. 'Go now!' she said. 'Quickly! Go!'

The nurse came into the room. 'Your mother is coming!' she said.

'Goodbye, my love,' Romeo said. 'Give me one kiss and I will go.'

'I am afraid,' Juliet said to her nurse as he left. 'I dreamed I saw Romeo at the bottom of a tomb. Oh, please let him come back to me!'

Lady Capulet entered Juliet's room. She and her husband had decided that they wanted Juliet to marry Paris.

'Daughter, why are you still in bed?' she asked.

'I am not well,' Juliet replied.

'You are still weeping because of Tybalt's death,' her mother said. 'It is wrong that his murderer is still alive. I will tell a friend in Mantua about Tybalt's death, and he will kill Romeo.'

Juliet did not want her mother to know about her marriage to Romeo, so she said, 'I will never be happy until I see Romeo again and he is punished for the death of my cousin.'

'My child,' Lady Capulet said, 'Let us think of happier things. Early on Thursday morning, Count Paris will marry you at St Peter's Church.'

'He will not!' cried Juliet. 'Tell my father it is too soon. I will not marry yet.'

'Here comes your father. Tell him yourself.'

Lord Capulet came into the room. 'What is wrong?' he said. 'Are you still weeping? Has your mother told you about your wedding to Paris?'

'Yes, sir,' said Lady Capulet. 'I told her, but she will not obey.'

'I do not understand. She should thank us. We have found her a fine husband.'

'I cannot thank you for something that I will hate,' said Juliet.

Lord Capulet was very angry. 'On Thursday, you will go with Paris to St Peter's Church, or I will take you there by force.'

'Please, father—,' Juliet cried.

'Go to the church on Thursday, or I will never speak to you again. You will not come into my house. You can beg and die in the streets.'

He left the room.

'Is there no pity?' said Juliet. 'Oh, my sweet mother. I beg you to delay this marriage for a month, a week. If you do not, I will die like Tybalt.'

'That is enough. I will not help you,' Lady Capulet said, and she left the room.

'Nurse, what can I do?' Juliet cried.'Help me!'

'Your mother is right,' the nurse said.'You should marry Paris. He is a good man.You will be happy with him.'

'I will go to Friar Lawrence. Tell my mother that I am sorry my father is upset.'The nurse went out.

'If he cannot help me, I will end my life,' Juliet thought.

◆

Paris was in Friar Lawrence's cell.'I want to arrange my marriage to Juliet,' he said.

'On Thursday, sir?' said the friar.'That is very soon.'

'Capulet wants us to marry quickly, and that is my wish too. Juliet weeps too much because of Tybalt's death. Her wedding will stop her tears.'

'I must delay this wedding,' thought the friar.'It should never take place at all.'

Then he said to Paris,'Look, sir, here she comes!'

'My lady and my wife,' said Paris.

'I am not your wife yet,' said Juliet.

'I will make you my wife on Thursday. Until then, goodbye.' He went out and left Juliet alone with the friar.

'Oh, shut the door,' she cried,'and then come and weep with me. Nobody can help me! Nobody can offer me hope! If you cannot think of a plan to help me, I want to die.'

'Wait, daughter,' the friar said.'I think I can help.You say that you will kill yourself if you have to marry Paris. Then perhaps you can pretend to be dead for a short time.'

'I will do anything if I can stay true to my dear love, Romeo.'

'Go home. Tell your mother and father that you will marry Paris. Tomorrow is Wednesday. Go to bed alone tomorrow night. Don't let your nurse stay with you. When you are in bed, drink

'I will do anything if I can stay true to my dear love, Romeo.'

this liquid. You will feel cold and sleepy. Your skin will grow pale and you will not breathe. For forty-two hours you will seem to be dead. When Paris comes for you, he will think that you are dead. They will put you in your family's tomb.

'I will send a letter to Romeo. At the end of the forty-two hours, you will wake up and Romeo will take you away to Mantua. Are you brave enough to do this, or will fear stop you drinking the liquid?'

'Give me the drink. Don't speak of fear!' said Juliet.

'I will send Friar John to Romeo with a letter,' the friar said.

Juliet went home. 'I am sorry that I refused to marry Paris,' she said to her father. 'I was wrong. Let us prepare for the wedding.'

◆

The next night, Juliet asked her nurse to leave the room.

'I am afraid,' she thought. 'What will happen if this liquid does not work? I am afraid that I will wake up before Romeo comes to me in the tomb. Romeo, Romeo, I am drinking this for you!'

Then she drank Friar Lawrence's liquid and fell back on her bed.

◆

The Capulets prepared for the wedding, and on the Thursday morning, Juliet's nurse came to wake her.

She called her name. 'Are you still asleep? Come, my lady, wake up.' At last she shook Juliet. 'Lady! Lady! Oh! Help! Help! My lady is dead!'

Juliet's parents heard her cries and ran into the room. Paris and Friar Lawrence were with them.

'Is Juliet ready to go to the church?' Friar Lawrence asked.

'She is ready to go,' Lord Capulet cried, 'but she will never return. Death has taken her.'

'She was a lovely young woman,' the friar said. 'Heaven wanted to share her with you. You could not stop her death. She is above the clouds in heaven. You must not weep now. Dry your tears and take her to the tomb.'

'We have flowers and music for her wedding,' said Lord Capulet sadly. 'Now we will use them for her tomb.'

So they took Juliet to the tomb of the Capulets.

◆

Romeo was far away in Mantua.

'I had a strange dream last night,' he remembered. 'I dreamed that Juliet came and found me dead. She kissed me and I was alive again.'

He saw his servant Balthazar coming towards him.

'Do you have any news from Verona?' he asked. 'How is my love? Is she well?'

But Balthazar answered, 'Her body is sleeping in the tomb of the Capulets. She is alive in heaven now.'

'What?' cried Romeo. 'Do you have a letter for me from the friar?'

'No.'

'Find me some horses. I must leave here tonight. Tonight I will lie with Juliet in her tomb.'

Balthazar was afraid. What was his master going to do?

Romeo went to a very poor chemist. This chemist sold medicines, but he needed more money so he also sold poison.

'If I pay this chemist with gold,' Romeo thought, 'he will give me a poison that will end my life.'

'Drink this poison. It will kill you immediately,' the chemist said.

'Buy food with my gold,' said Romeo, and he picked up the poisoned liquid.

◆

Friar John returned to Friar Lawrence.

'Welcome,' said Friar Lawrence. 'What does Romeo say?'

Friar John looked very unhappy. 'I could not go to Mantua,' he said. 'I went to a house in Verona, looking for a friar to go with me. While I was there, officers came and locked all the doors and windows. They thought that there was a dangerous illness in the house. They did not let anyone in or out, and nobody wanted to touch your letter. Here it is.'

'This is terrible!' said Friar Lawrence. 'Go quickly! Bring an iron stick to my cell.'

'In three hours Juliet will wake up,' he thought. 'I will write to Mantua. But I must open the tomb and hide Juliet in my cell until Romeo arrives.'

◆

Paris went to the Capulets' tomb, because he wanted to put flowers on it for Juliet. He heard people near the tomb and hid.

It was Romeo and Balthazar. 'Take this letter to my father,' Romeo said to his servant. 'Give me your lamp. I am going to say goodbye to my lady Juliet. Now go away.'

But Balthazar thought, 'I will hide near here. My master looks strange. What is he going to do?'

Paris heard a noise as Romeo broke open the tomb.

'It is Romeo!' he cried. 'What evil is he doing to the dead bodies? Romeo, I have caught you! You must die.'

'Yes, I must die,' said Romeo. 'That is why I am here. I came to kill myself. I do not want to hurt you, boy. Go away, and say that a madman told you to leave.'

But Paris made Romeo fight. Paris's servant ran to call the officers who were on guard through the night.

Romeo's sword wounded Paris.

'I am dying!' Paris cried. 'Place me in the tomb with Juliet.'

Romeo looked at the face of the dead man. 'It is Count Paris, one of Mercutio's family. Poor young man. I will put you in the tomb.'

He opened Juliet's tomb and looked at her face.

'Dear Juliet,' he said. 'Why are you still so beautiful? Is death keeping you here as his lover? Let me look at you again. Let my arms hold you for the last time. I will stay here with you forever.' He drank the poison. 'This poison acts quickly. With this kiss, I will die.'

Friar Lawrence came running towards the tomb. He saw Balthazar, and then he saw a light inside.

'Romeo, my master, has been in the tomb for more than half an hour,' Balthazar said.

Full of fear, the friar went into the tomb. He saw the dead bodies of Romeo and Paris, and at that moment, Juliet woke up.

'Where is my Romeo?' she asked.

'Lady,' said the friar, 'come out of this place of death. A greater power than ours has ruined all our plans. Your husband is dead and Paris, too. We can do nothing here. Come away with me. I will take you to a safe place.'

'Go! Leave this place. I will stay,' said Juliet.

The friar hurried away to find someone to help him.

Juliet looked at Romeo. 'What is this?' she asked herself. 'There is a cup in my true love's hand. Poison? Oh, Romeo, you have drunk it all and left none for me. I will kiss your lips; perhaps there is some poison on them.'

She kissed him, but then she heard the guards arrive. There was no more time. Juliet took Romeo's dagger and pushed it into her own heart.

The prince and his servants arrived at the tomb, followed by the Capulets and Montagues. The guards caught the weeping friar.

'What happened?' Prince Escalus asked. 'Why have you called me from my bed?'

'Some people in the street are crying, "Romeo!". Some are crying, "Juliet!", and some are crying, "Paris!",' Lady Capulet said. 'They are shouting and running towards our tomb.'

'*Romeo is dead, and Juliet has killed herself.*'

Then a guard told them, 'Count Paris is dead, Romeo is dead, and Juliet has killed herself.'

'Here is the friar,' said another guard, 'and here is Romeo's servant, Balthazar.'

'Prince, my wife died during the night,' Lord Montague said. 'She was very sad when my son left the city. Her sadness killed her.'

The prince turned to the friar. 'Tell me, Friar, what do you know about all this?'

The friar, in a few words, told the whole unhappy story. 'If these deaths are my fault, then punish me with death.'

'I know that you are a good man,' said the prince. 'Where is Romeo's servant? What can he tell us?'

'I told my master that Juliet was dead,' Balthazar said. 'He came here and told me to go away. He said he would kill me if I stayed.'

Paris's servant also told his story. 'My master came to put flowers on Juliet's tomb. He saw somebody and pulled out his sword. I ran away to find the guards.'

'Capulet, Montague,' the prince said sadly. 'These terrible things happened because your families hate each other. And I have also lost two members of my family.'

Capulet said to Montague, 'My daughter's marriage with your son, Romeo, has joined our families at last. Oh, brother Montague, give me your hand.'

'And so,' the prince said, 'this dark and cloudy morning has brought a sad peace. There will never be a sadder story than the story of Romeo and Juliet.'

Macbeth

At the time of this story, Duncan was the King of Scotland. Macbeth was a great lord and the leader of the Scottish army. Banquo was also a lord and an army leader.

Macbeth had won a great battle against an army from Norway. He and Banquo were coming back from the battle, riding over some wild, open land in a storm. In the wildest part they saw three witches sitting around a fire. The witches stopped the two men.

'Who are you?' asked Banquo. 'You look like women, but you have beards.'

'Speak!' said Macbeth. 'What are you?'

'Greetings, Macbeth, Lord of Glamis,' the first witch said.

'Greetings, Macbeth, Lord of Cawdor,' the second witch said.

'Greetings, Macbeth. You will be king,' the third witch said.

Then they turned to Banquo.

'You will not be king,' the third witch said. 'But your children and your grandchildren will become kings.'

Macbeth and Banquo rode away from the witches.

'I am already Lord of Glamis,' said Macbeth, 'but how can I become Lord of Cawdor? The Lord of Cawdor is still alive. And I do not believe that I will be king. They said your children will become kings, Banquo.'

At that moment, messengers from King Duncan came to Macbeth.

'The Lord of Cawdor helped the Norwegians,' one of them said. 'He fought against the king. Now the king wants you to be the new Lord of Cawdor.'

'Lord of Glamis and Lord of Cawdor,' Macbeth said to Banquo with surprise.

'If you believe the witches, you will become king,' said Banquo.

'Perhaps these witches are telling the truth – and perhaps they want to cause trouble and death.'

◆

In Macbeth's castle, Lady Macbeth read a letter from her husband.

'The witches say that my husband will be king,' she thought. 'But Macbeth is too kind, too gentle. There are things that he must do, but he is afraid to do them. I must speak to him, and make him brave.'

Then Macbeth arrived at the castle. 'My dearest love, the king is coming here tonight,' he said. 'He wants to honour me.'

'When will he leave?'

'He says that he will leave tomorrow.'

'Oh, no! He must never leave! Macbeth, your face shows your thoughts and feelings. You must hide them. Leave everything to me.'

◆

King Duncan arrived at Macbeth's castle with his two sons, Malcolm and Donalbain. After dinner, Macbeth came out of the dining hall.

'If I want to be king, I must kill King Duncan,' he said to himself. 'I must kill him quickly. But what will happen if I kill him? An act of this kind could harm me. The king is a guest in my house, so I should guard him against murderers, not kill him. Duncan is a good king and his death will cause great sorrow. No! I will not do it.'

Just then, Lady Macbeth came out of the dining hall. 'Why did you leave the room?' she asked.

'I do not want to kill the king,' said Macbeth. 'He is good to me. People like and admire me. I will not throw away their good opinion.'

Lady Macbeth was very angry with her husband. 'What are

you saying?' she asked. 'Why are you so afraid? You want to be king. Are you afraid to kill him?'

'I am a brave man,' Macbeth replied. 'I will do everything that a man should do – everything that is right.'

'You must be strong,' Lady Macbeth said.

'But what will happen if we fail?'

'Then we fail!' said Lady Macbeth. 'But if you are brave, we will succeed. Wait until Duncan is asleep. We will make everyone believe that the king's servants killed him. I will put something in their drink to make them sleep, and we will cover them with the king's blood.'

'Yes, we will do it,' said Macbeth. 'But we must look kind and happy, so no one knows our plans.'

The king and his two sons came out of the dining hall. The king was tired so he went to bed early.

Later that night, Banquo and his son Fleance met Macbeth in the garden of the castle.

'Here is a beautiful jewel from the king to your wife,' said Banquo. 'He has gone to bed.'

◆

Midnight came. Lady Macbeth made the king's servants drunk, so they knew nothing. She took her dagger and went to the king's bedroom. Duncan was sleeping deeply after his long journey. His face reminded Lady Macbeth of her father and she could not kill him, so she left.

Macbeth looked at the dagger in his hand. 'The witches told the truth. I must go into Duncan's room and kill him,' he thought.

When he came out of the king's room, he saw his wife. 'I have done it,' he said. 'Did you hear anything? Did you speak? I thought I heard a voice. "Macbeth has murdered sleep," it said. "He will never sleep again."'

'I heard nothing,' Lady Macbeth said. 'You imagined it.

Now, get some water and wash the blood from your hands. Why did you bring the dagger here? You must leave it in the king's bedroom. Take it back and cover the sleeping servants with blood.'

'I cannot go into that room and see the king's body again,' Macbeth said. 'I am afraid.'

'You are weak,' said Lady Macbeth. 'Give me the dagger. I will spread blood on the servants.'

When she came back, she showed her hands to Macbeth. 'Now look! My hands are as red as yours. But my heart is not as white with fear as your heart. Put on your night clothes. We want people to think that we are asleep.'

Suddenly there was a loud knock on the great gate of the castle.

'What is that?' cried Macbeth. 'Every noise frightens me.' He looked at his bloody hands. 'My hands! All the water in the oceans will not clean the blood from these hands!'

People were still beating on the gate. Macduff and Lennox, two Scottish lords, had arrived. Macbeth came out to greet them.

'Is the king awake?' asked Macduff.

'Not yet, but I will take you to his room.'

Macduff went into the king's room. A moment later, he ran out with a loud cry.

'What is the matter?' Lennox asked.

'It is too horrible!' Macduff cried. 'Quickly, wake Malcolm and Donalbain. Ring the castle bell.' Banquo came in. 'Oh, Banquo, Banquo!' cried Macduff. 'Our king is dead.'

Malcolm and Donalbain came out of their rooms.

'What is the matter?' Donalbain asked.

'Your father, the king, is dead!' Lennox said. 'We think his servants murdered him. They are covered with blood.'

'We must ask questions and try to find the answers,' Banquo said. 'This is a bloody piece of work. What does it mean?'

The king's two sons were afraid. Who could they trust?

'I will go to England,' said Malcolm. 'Someone in this castle murdered our father. They are only pretending to be sad.'

'And I will go to Ireland,' said Donalbain. 'We will be safer in different countries.'

◆

After that night, strange and frightening things happened in Scotland. There was black fear in everyone's heart.

Banquo did not trust Macbeth. 'Now Macbeth has everything,' he said to himself. 'The death of Duncan makes him king. King, Cawdor, Glamis – he is everything that the witches promised. But they promised something for me too. I will be the father of kings. Will that be true?'

Macbeth and Lady Macbeth invited people to a feast.

Macbeth and Lady Macbeth invited people to a feast.

'Fleance and I must ride out this afternoon,' Banquo said. 'But we will be back for the feast.'

'Good,' Macbeth replied. 'I hear that Duncan's sons, in England and Ireland, are telling lies about their father's murderer.'

When the room was empty, Macbeth called a servant. 'Bring in the two men who are waiting outside the palace gate,' he said.

'The witches said that Banquo's sons would be kings of Scotland,' he said to himself. 'I have done this terrible thing for Banquo and his children, not for myself. He must die, and Fleance, his son, must die too.'

The two men came in. They were murderers.

'Banquo is your enemy,' Macbeth said. 'He is my enemy, too. You must kill him. I will tell you where you can wait to catch him and his son.'

◆

Before the feast began, Lady Macbeth talked to her husband.

'You spend too much time alone,' she said. 'Your only friends are your sad thoughts. It is too late to worry. Duncan is dead.'

'We are still in danger,' Macbeth replied. 'We both have terrible dreams every night. I am full of fear while the dead rest in peace.'

'Don't let anyone see that you are worried,' said his wife. 'Look happy when our guests come here tonight.'

'Yes, I will,' Macbeth said. 'And before night falls, something will happen. When you know what it is, you will say to me, "Well done!"'

◆

But the two murderers had only carried out half of Macbeth's plan. They had killed Banquo, but Fleance escaped. One of the murderers returned at dinner time, when the lords and ladies were enjoying the feast.

'There is blood on your face,' Macbeth said to him.

'It is Banquo's blood,' the murderer replied. 'But I have bad news. Fleance is still alive.'

'Now I am still afraid,' Macbeth said to himself. He moved away from his guests and stood thinking.

'Sit down,' Lady Macbeth said. 'These people in the hall will notice your strange behaviour. Be happy among your friends!'

There was one empty seat at the table. Quietly the bloody ghost of the murdered Banquo sat down in it.

Ross, one of the lords, said to Macbeth, 'Won't you sit down with us? Here is an empty place.'

But Macbeth saw the ghost of Banquo in the chair. 'The table is full,' he said. 'Who did this?' His face was white with fear. No one else could see the ghost, so no one understood his words. 'You cannot say that I did it!' Macbeth cried to the ghost. 'Don't shake your bloody hair at me!'

Macbeth saw the ghost of Banquo in the chair.

'My lord is often like this,' Lady Macbeth said to the guests. 'It is nothing. He will soon be well.'

In a low voice, Macbeth spoke to his wife. 'I have seen Banquo!' he said.

She was angry with him. 'You are looking at an empty chair!'

But the ghost appeared again to Macbeth.

'Look! He is there!' Macbeth cried.

Lady Macbeth could do nothing, so she asked everyone to leave. 'My husband is getting worse,' she told her guests.

'The ghost demands blood,' said Macbeth. 'Blood demands blood. Tomorrow I will go and see the three witches. I must know what will happen.'

'You need sleep,' said Lady Macbeth. 'Come, we will sleep.'

◆

In the same wild place, the three witches were singing strange songs and putting mysterious things into a pot over a fire. They were making black magic.

Then they suddenly stopped. 'He's coming,' one of them said.

Macbeth stood there, looking at them. 'Give me answers to my questions,' he said.

'Speak!' said the first witch.

'Ask!' said the second witch.

'We will answer,' said the third witch. 'Do you want to hear the words from our mouths or from the mouths of our masters?'

'Call your masters!' Macbeth cried. 'Let me see them.'

Macbeth began to see strange and unreal things. Ghosts appeared in front of him.

The first ghost was the head of a soldier. It said, 'Macbeth! Macbeth! Watch Macduff. Watch him and protect yourself from him.'

'I do not know who you are,' Macbeth said. 'But thank you for your good advice.'

The second ghost was a child covered in blood. It said, 'Macbeth! Be brave! You cannot be hurt by any man who was born from a woman.'

The third ghost was a child wearing a crown. It carried a small tree in its hand. 'Be brave,' it said. 'Be proud, and do not worry. Your enemies will never beat you until Birnam Wood moves to Dunsinane Hill.'

Macbeth felt happier now. 'I was afraid of Macduff before,' he thought. 'Now I will make sure that he does not harm me. And how can the last two things ever happen? I am safe!'

He turned to the witches. 'Can you tell me if Banquo's children will be kings of this country?' he asked.

'Do not ask us any more questions,' the witches said.

'Answer me or I will curse you!' Macbeth cried.

Eight kings appeared, and then a figure like Banquo.

'Banquo is covered in blood,' cried Macbeth. 'He is pointing at them, showing me that they are his sons. I do not want to see any more!'

The witches danced around and then they disappeared.

Later, Macbeth heard that Macduff had run away to England.

'I know what to do,' Macbeth thought. 'I will burn down his castle and kill his wife and all his children.'

◆

In England, Macduff was talking to King Duncan's son, Malcolm. 'When will these terrible things in Scotland end?' asked Malcolm.

Then Ross, another Scottish lord, came to see them.

'What is happening in Scotland?' asked Macduff.

'I have bad news,' answered Ross. 'Each day brings more sadness and trouble.'

'Go home,' said Malcolm. 'Tell my people that we will come very soon. The English have given me 10,000 men. We are coming to fight Macbeth.'

'That is good news,' said Ross. 'But I must give you bad news, Macduff. Something terrible has happened. Macbeth has taken your castle. He has killed your wife and all your children.'

'What! All my pretty children? Did you say all? And their mother?' Macduff cried.

'Your wife, children, servants – everyone that he could find in the castle,' Ross said.

'And I was not there,' said Macduff. 'Kind heavens, bring me face to face with this murderer. Now he will never escape me!'

◆

Lady Macbeth was ill. Her servant spoke to the doctor.

'She cannot sleep. The king has gone away to fight against Macduff and Malcolm. Every night my lady gets up from her bed. She puts on her coat, takes some paper, writes on it and then goes back to bed. She does all these things in her sleep. She does not know what she is doing.'

'What does she say?' asked the doctor.

'I do not want to repeat her words,' the servant said.

As she spoke, Lady Macbeth walked slowly into the room, carrying a lamp.

'She hates to be in the dark,' said the lady. 'She always has a lamp by her side.'

'Her eyes are open,' said the doctor. 'What is she doing with her hands?'

'She does that very often, sometimes for a quarter of an hour. She is trying to wash her hands.'

'Listen!' said the doctor. 'She is speaking. I will write down her words.'

'There is still blood here on my hands,' Lady Macbeth said. 'Here is more blood. I did not know that an old man had so much blood in him. Will these hands never be clean? Wash your hands, put on your night clothes. Banquo is dead. He cannot come out of

Lady Macbeth walked slowly into the room . . .

his tomb. Someone is knocking at the gate! Go to bed!'

'I have heard enough,' the doctor said. 'I cannot help her. Only the gods can help her now.'

◆

Soon everyone knew that a great English army was on its way. The Scottish lords rode with the army and talked about their king, Macbeth.

'Some say that he is mad,' said one.

'His men do not love or trust him. They act only because he orders them to act. His title of king means nothing. It is like a big man's coat worn by a little thief,' said another.

'Well, let us march on towards Birnam!'

Macbeth's mind was sick, but he still felt safe. 'They cannot hurt me,' he said to himself. 'How can Birnam Wood move to Dunsinane? How can I die at the hands of a man who was not born from a woman? Malcolm was born from a woman.'

Soon Malcolm, Macduff and their soldiers were riding near Birnam Wood.

'Tell each soldier to take a branch from a tree and hide behind it,' Malcolm said. 'Then Macbeth will not see us.'

Back in the castle, Macbeth heard the sound of women crying. He called a servant.

'Why are people crying?' he asked.

'The queen is dead, my lord.'

'This is not a good time for her to die,' Macbeth. 'I cannot think about it now.'

A messenger came running in.

'You have come to tell me something. Tell me quickly!' cried Macbeth.

'My good lord,' the messenger said. 'I have just seen something very strange. I was standing on guard and I looked towards Birnam – and the forest began to move!'

'If you are lying to me,' said Macbeth, 'I will hang you from the nearest tree until you are dead.'

But it was true. The soldiers were carrying branches in front of them as they walked. Nobody knew how many men were moving towards Dunsinane.

Macbeth still felt that he was safe. Every man was born from a woman!

He heard wild shouts and the noise of sword striking sword. He heard the cries of dying men and the shouts of his enemies.

Suddenly Macduff stood in front of him. 'Macbeth, you killed all the people that I love,' he cried. 'Show me your face!'

'Move back!' said Macbeth. 'I have already killed too many of your family.' But Macduff was not listening. He was there to kill Macbeth. 'You are wasting your time!' cried Macbeth. 'No man can kill me except one who was not born from a woman!'

'Let me tell you, then,' cried Macduff. 'I was cut from my mother's body early. I was not born in the normal way.'

Macbeth knew then that he would die. But he was a brave man in this final battle. 'Come! We will fight to the end,' he shouted. 'And there will be a curse on the first man who cries, "Stop! Enough!"'

Macduff's anger made him strong and he killed Macbeth. Then he cut off Macbeth's head and showed it to the English army, the Scottish lords and their soldiers.

Malcolm, their new king, said, 'I thank you all from my heart for helping me.'

The tired men went home. Soon, they all came together again at Scone, to see the crown of Scotland put on the head of their new young king.

King Lear

King Lear, King of Britain, came into the hall with his three daughters: Goneril, who was married to the Duke of Albany; Regan, who was married to the Duke of Cornwall, and Cordelia. Cordelia was not yet married, but the King of France hoped to make her his wife.

The king spread out a map. 'I have separated my kingdom into three parts,' he said. 'I am old, and I do not want to govern my kingdom any longer. Let younger people do the work. So I will give the best part of my kingdom to the daughter who loves me most. Goneril, you are my eldest daughter. You must speak first.'

King Lear, King of Britain, came into the hall with his three daughters.

'Sir,' said Goneril, 'I love you as much as I love my life, my health, my beauty and my honour. I love you as much as any daughter can ever love her father. I cannot put into words how much I love you.'

'What shall I say?' thought Cordelia. 'I love him, but I cannot say such things.'

King Lear was very pleased with Goneril's speech. He said to her, 'I will give all the land between these two lines on the map to you, your husband and your children. Now, what does my second daughter, Regan, say?'

'I love you as much as my sister,' Regan replied. 'But she has not said enough. Nothing pleases me except my love for you. My only happiness comes from my love for you.'

The king was pleased with Regan's reply and he gave a third of his kingdom to her.

Then it was Cordelia's turn to speak. 'Now,' said her father, 'what do you say? Shall I give you the richest part of my kingdom? Shall I give you more than I gave to your sisters? Speak!'

Cordelia answered, 'I can say nothing, my lord.'

'Nothing?' the king asked. He was surprised by her words.

'Nothing,' she said.

'Nothing will bring you nothing. Speak again.'

'I cannot put my feelings into words,' Cordelia said. 'I love you as much as any daughter can love her father. You are my father: you gave me life, cared for me, loved me. So of course I love you. I obey you. I honour you. Why do my sisters have husbands if you have all their love? When I marry, I will give my husband half my love.'

'Do you really mean that?' Lear asked. 'You are very young and unkind.'

'I am young, my lord, but I am telling you the truth.'

'Truth? Then you will only receive truth. From today I will not be your father. You will be a stranger to me and to my heart.

Cornwall and Albany, you can have Cordelia's share of my kingdom. I will stay with each of you for one month. I will only bring 100 knights with me. People will still call me king, but you will share the government of all my lands.'

The King of France came in.

'I do not want you to take Cordelia as your wife,' Lear said to him. 'You should look for a better woman.'

'This is very strange,' said the King of France. 'She was your favourite daughter. Why have you changed your mind about her?'

'Tell the king that I have lost my father's love because I do not have a tongue like my sisters. I am glad that I do not speak like them,' interrupted Cordelia.

'You have not pleased me,' Lear said. 'You are not my daughter. Why were you ever born?'

But the King of France loved Cordelia. 'Fair Cordelia, your father refuses to keep you, but I love you. Your loneliness makes you even lovelier to me. You are a good woman. I will happily marry you. I will make you the queen of my heart and queen of my lovely country. Say goodbye to your father, the king. Better things are waiting for you.'

Cordelia said goodbye to her father. Then she turned to her sisters. 'I know what you are doing!' she said. 'Take care of our father.'

'Do not tell us our duty!' said Regan.

'Look after your lord of France. He is marrying you because he pities you,' said Goneril.

'You are clever and you hide your faults. In time, people will see the truth,' Cordelia replied.

'Come, Cordelia,' said the King of France, and they left the castle.

'Sister,' said Goneril, 'I suppose our father will stay with me tonight.'

'Yes, he will. And next month he will come to us.'

'You see how he changes his mind. He always loved Cordelia most. He was foolish to throw her out now. As he grows older, he will become more and more difficult. We must be ready for that.'

◆

The Earl of Gloucester was a great lord. He had two sons, Edgar and Edmund. Edgar was his true son from his marriage, and Edmund was the earl's bastard, Edgar's half-brother. Edmund hated Edgar.

At that moment, Edmund was in a room in Gloucester's castle.

'There should be no difference between Edgar and me,' he thought. 'Why do people think that he is more important than I am? My body is as strong as his. My mind is as clear as his. But he is the next Earl of Gloucester and he will get all our father's land. Well, Edgar, *I* will get the land. At the moment my father loves us equally, so I must make him hate you.' He looked at a letter in his hand. It was part of his plot to destroy Edgar.

Just then his father, Gloucester, entered. Edmund pretended to hide the letter.

'Why are you trying to hide that letter?' asked Gloucester.

'It is a letter from my brother Edgar,' Edmund said. 'I have not finished reading it. I do not think that you ought to read it.'

'Give me the letter. Let me see it,' Gloucester said.

He read:

> *We will not get our money until we are too old to enjoy it.*
> *Come to me and I will tell you more. If our father dies soon,*
> *I will let you have half of his money. You will be a rich man.*
> *And you will earn the love of your brother,*
> *Edgar*

'My son Edgar! Did he write this letter? How did you get it?' Gloucester asked.

'My lord, someone passed it in through my window. Edgar believes that it is wrong for sons to wait until their fathers die of old age. I have often heard him say that.'

'That seems to be what he says in his letter! He is evil! Go and find him. Where is he?'

'I do not know,' said Edmund. 'But please do not do anything to my brother. Wait until you can prove it. What does he intend to do? I will try to find out for you.'

'Edmund, find him. Make him trust you and tell you his plans.'

Gloucester left the room. Soon Edmund saw Edgar coming towards him.

'Have you seen my father?' he asked Edgar.

'I saw him last night,' Edgar said.

'Did you talk?'

'Yes, for two hours,' said Edgar.

'Did you end the conversation as good friends? Was he angry with you?' Edmund asked.

'No,' said Edgar. 'Why?'

'Because he is very angry with you now,' said Edmund. 'I am afraid that you are in danger.'

'An evil person has spoken against me,' Edgar said.

'I am afraid that is true, brother. Go to my room. At the right time, I will take you to Lord Gloucester. You can speak to him then.'

Edgar left and Edmund smiled to himself. 'My father believes everything I say. My brother is a good man and he thinks no one could plot against him. I am clever and I will get everything that I want – everything that my birth has taken away from me.'

◆

King Lear was foolish to trust Goneril. He stayed in her house with his 100 knights, but he was a difficult visitor. Now Goneril had power over him, and she became an unkind daughter.

'Behave coldly when you see him,' she said to her servant. 'Tell all my servants to be unfriendly with his knights. I am going to write to my sister. She and I agree that we do not want our father to stay with us. She will behave in the same way.'

Lear came into the room. 'You look angry, daughter,' he said. 'You often look angry. Why?'

'Your knights are always quarrelling,' Goneril answered. 'They make a lot of noise. My house is in disorder. It is too much! I will not allow it! I have spoken to you about this before. I believe that you tell them to behave badly. I cannot stop them because you are their master. I am your daughter, but I must speak.'

'Are you my daughter?'

'Listen, sir,' said Goneril. 'Be sensible! Recently you have changed. What are these feelings that have changed you? Be the man you really are.'

'Who can tell me what I really am?' cried Lear. 'I really thought that I had daughters.'

'You are old,' said Goneril, 'and you should be wise. But you keep 100 knights and their followers here in my house and they behave badly. I beg you, send some of your knights away. Keep just a few men. They should be wise and older men like you.'

'Darkness and devils! Bring my horse and call my men. You are an unnatural child! I will not trouble you any more! I still have one daughter left. I was mad – I made a mistake when I trusted you.'

Lear went out, and Goneril heard him shout in surprise.

'What? She has already sent away fifty of my knights? But I have another daughter. I am sure that she will be kind. When she hears this, she will hit Goneril's face with her own fingers.'

◆

In the Earl of Gloucester's castle, Edmund called Edgar to him. He knew that their father was in the next room. The two brothers talked for a minute, and then Edmund said, 'My father is coming! I can hear him.'

He lowered his voice to a whisper. 'He has ordered me to make you a prisoner. I must pretend to pull out my sword and attack you. You must pretend to defend yourself.'

Their swords struck each other. Then Edmund whispered, 'Now escape! Run away, quickly!'

Edgar ran out.

Edmund struck his own arm with his sword and wounded himself. 'Father! Father!' he cried.

Gloucester came in. 'Where is he, Edmund?'

'Look, sir! I am bleeding. Edgar told me to murder you. When I refused, he attacked and wounded me. He was frightened by the noise I made, so he ran away.'

'We must find him immediately!' said Gloucester.

'I tried to make him give up his plot against you but I failed,' Edmund said. 'Then I said that I would tell you. He said, "You poor bastard, no one will believe you." He said that you loved him. You would not believe that he wrote the letter or plotted against you.'

'How could he say that it was not his letter?' Gloucester asked. 'I will send a picture of him to every part of the kingdom. I will make sure that he does not escape. Edmund, you are my good son. You will have all my land when I die.'

Cornwall and Regan entered the room. They had come to visit Gloucester.

Cornwall said to Gloucester, 'We have heard strange things about your son Edgar. Did he really want to kill you?'

'Oh!' cried Gloucester. 'My old heart is broken! I am ashamed that you know about this.'

'Wasn't Edgar a friend of those knights who came to my house with my father?' asked Regan.

'I do not know,' said Gloucester.

'Yes,' said Edmund. 'He was.'

'Then I am not surprised,' said Regan. 'They advised Edgar to kill you, Gloucester. They wanted to get your money. My sister sent me a letter about those knights. If my father brings them to my house, I will not be there.'

◆

When Lear arrived at Gloucester's castle, Gloucester came out and spoke to him.

'Do my daughter and Cornwall really refuse to speak to me?' Lear said. 'You say that they are sick. You say that they are tired, that they travelled all night! I do not believe it. I, the king, wish to speak to Cornwall. I wish to speak to my daughter. Tell them to come out to me now!'

'I wish there was no trouble between you,' said Gloucester, as he went into the castle.

'Oh, my heart! My heart!' cried Lear. 'Do not break!'

Gloucester came back with Cornwall, Regan and their servants.

'Good morning to you both,' Lear said.

'I am happy to see you,' Regan replied.

'Of course you are happy to see me. I am your father,' said Lear. 'Dear Regan, your sister has been so unkind to me.'

'I cannot believe that my sister failed in her duty to you. You must not blame her. She only tried to make your noisy followers behave. You are old, sir. We know your needs better than you do. Let us help you. Please, sir, say that you were wrong. Go back and ask Goneril to forgive you.'

'Ask her to forgive me!' cried Lear. 'Do you want me to go to her and say, "Dear daughter, I am old. I beg you to give me clothes and a bed and food."? Never! She sent away half my knights. Let heaven strike her!'

'Will you curse me like that when you are angry?' said Regan.

'Oh, never, Regan! You are kind and gentle. You will never hurt me. You have kind eyes, not cold eyes like hers. You will not forget that I gave you half my kingdom.'

Just then, Goneril arrived.

'Aren't you ashamed to see me?' said Lear. 'And you, Regan! Why are you taking her hand?'

'Please, father, go back and stay with my sister until the end of the month,' said Regan.

'Return to Goneril? Without my knights? Never! I will live in the open air without a roof.'

'If that is what you want, then do it, sir,' said Goneril.

'Please, daughter, do not make me mad. I will not trouble you again, my child. Goodbye. We do not have to meet again. I can stay with Regan.'

'No, sir,' said Regan. 'I did not expect you. I am not ready for your visit. You have fifty followers! One house cannot hold so many knights. Bring twenty-five. You do not need more. My servants can look after you.'

'Why does he need twenty-five knights?' Goneril asked. 'Why does he need ten? Or five?'

'Why does he need any followers?' said Regan.

'The poorest people have more than they need to keep them alive,' Lear said. 'Oh, you gods, help me. Make me angry. Daughters, I will do terrible things to you both! Do you think you will make me weep? No, I will not weep. My heart will break into a thousand pieces before I weep. Oh, I will go mad!'

He went away, followed by Gloucester.

A storm began. 'We must go inside,' Cornwall said.

'This castle is too small to hold the old man and his knights,' Regan said.

'It is his fault. Let him suffer,' said Goneril.

'I will let him stay at my home,' Regan said. 'But not one of his followers will enter the house.'

Gloucester came back to them. 'The king is very angry. He has called for his horse. I do not know where he is going.'

'Shut your doors, Lord Gloucester,' said Cornwall. 'Come in out of the storm.'

◆

Gloucester's men were hunting Edgar. They watched all the roads, so he could not escape.

'I will put mud on my face,' he thought. 'My hair will be long and dirty and I will wear old clothes. The country is full of mad people, shouting and begging. They travel through the farms and villages. I will be one of them, and I will call myself Poor Tom.'

Lear was also caught in the storm. He was losing his mind, and sometimes he was completely mad. He began to talk to the weather.

'Fires of the stormy sky above me, burn my head of white hair! Thunder, you shake everything, but I do not care what you do to me. I did not give you my lands or call you my children. You do not have to give me anything. Here I stand, your servant, a poor, weak old man. But do not join my two daughters and fight against an old man. Oh, here is a hut. I can rest here until my daughters come to apologize.'

Edgar was inside the hut. He came out, pretending to be a madman. 'Oh! Oh!' he cried. 'Poor Tom is cold! The devil has led him through fire and through water. The devil has put knives in his bed, and poison in his food. Poor Tom!'

'What! Did you give everything to your two daughters?' Lear asked.

'Poor Tom has no daughters,' Edgar said.

'Of course you have daughters. Only daughters can be so cruel. Come with me and we can talk about our cruel daughters.'

◆

Lear was also caught in the storm.

Gloucester left his castle and came to find the king. He found Lear and Edgar, but he did not recognize his son.

'King Lear, your daughters ordered me to close the doors of my castle against you,' he said. 'I cannot obey – their commands are too hard. I came to find you. Let me take you to a place where there is a warm fire and some food.'

Lear did not understand him and spoke wild, broken words.

'Ask him again, my lord Gloucester,' said Edgar. 'He is mad, just like Poor Tom.'

'Can you blame him?' Gloucester asked. 'His daughters want him to die. I am almost mad myself. I had a son once, and now he is a stranger to me. Not long ago, he wanted to kill me. I loved him so much.'

Gloucester led them to a room in a farmhouse near his castle. Then he went out to look for things to make the room more comfortable.

Soon he came back. 'There is a plot to kill the king,' he cried. 'Quick, take him towards Dover. You will find help there.'

They carried the sleeping old man away to Dover.

◆

In Gloucester's castle, Edmund was speaking to Cornwall. Edgar and Gloucester were, he said, both evil men.

'I discovered that my father is a traitor,' Edmund said. 'The French army is going to attack us. This letter shows that my father knows about the attack. He welcomes it!'

'Come with me,' said Cornwall. 'I will make you a very rich man.'

Cornwall found Goneril and Regan in another part of Gloucester's castle. He said to Goneril, 'Go quickly to your husband, Albany. Show him this letter. The French army has landed.' Then he said to his servants, 'Find the traitor Gloucester and bring him here.'

'Kill him!' said Regan.

'Take out his eyes!' said Goneril.

'Leave him to me,' answered Cornwall. Then he said to Edmund, 'Go with Goneril. I am going to punish your father, the traitor. I do not want you to watch.'

So Goneril and Edmund left.

Two or three men brought Gloucester to Cornwall and Regan.

'Tie his arms,' ordered Cornwall. 'Make sure that he cannot escape.'

'My friends,' cried Gloucester, 'what are you doing? You are guests in my house. Do not do this to me!'

But the servants tied him up. The evil Regan laughed. 'Tighter!' she cried. 'Don't be kind to him! He is a traitor.'

'I am not a traitor,' Gloucester cried.

Regan went to him and pulled his white beard.

'Now, sit,' said Cornwall. 'Tell me about the letters that came from France. And where is the mad king? Where did you send him?'

They turned Gloucester's simple, true answers against him.

'I am tied up like a poor animal,' Gloucester said. 'I sent the king to Dover. I do not want to see your evil fingers take out his poor old eyes. But I will see God punish you. You are evil children.'

'You are wrong! You will never see anything,' cried Cornwall. 'Men! Hold the chair! You will not see because I am going to take your eyes out!'

'Help! Help!' Gloucester shouted.

One of Cornwall's servants ran to stop his master. 'Stop!' he cried. 'I have served you for many years, but you must stop!'

'You dog!' cried Regan.

Cornwall pulled out his sword and attacked the servant. Regan took a sword from another man and wounded Cornwall's servant.

'Oh, my lord,' cried the dying servant to Gloucester, 'he will be punished. You will see.'

'He will see nothing!' said Cornwall, and he took out both Gloucester's eyes.

Gloucester screamed in pain. 'Where is my son Edmund? Edmund, help me!'

'Traitor!' said Regan. 'Edmund hates you. Edmund told us that you were helping the King of France.'

'I was wrong about Edgar!' Gloucester said. 'Edgar was my true and honest son. I was wrong not to trust him. Kind gods, forgive me, and help him.'

Regan said to the servants, 'Throw him out of the gates and let him smell his way to Dover.'

A man went out with the blind Gloucester. Regan went away with her husband, Cornwall. His servant had wounded him during the fight and he was bleeding.

◆

In a wild place, Edgar was walking alone.

'My life cannot get worse,' he thought. 'But that is better than living in fear. I can still hope and all changes will make my life better.'

He saw his father coming slowly towards him. An old man was leading him. He heard Gloucester say to the old man, 'Go away, good friend. You will suffer if people see you with me. You will get into trouble. You cannot help me.'

'You cannot see. What will you do?' asked the old man.

'When I could see, I made great mistakes. Oh, Edgar, Edgar! I want to live long enough to hold you in my arms again! Is someone there?'

'It is a mad beggar,' said the old man. 'It is poor, mad Tom.'

'Poor Tom is cold,' said Edgar. 'Your poor, sweet eyes! They are covered in blood!'

'Do you know the way to Dover, Poor Tom?' asked Gloucester.

'Yes, I know the way,' Tom replied.

'There is a rock at Dover, high above the sea. If you take me to the edge of it, I will give you a jewel. You will be a rich man.'

'Give me your arm. Poor Tom will lead you.'

◆

Goneril and Edmund were talking in front of Albany's castle when Goneril's servant came out to them.

'The Duke of Albany is behaving strangely,' the servant said. 'I tell him good things and he gets angry. I tell him bad things and he is pleased. I told him about the French army and he smiled. I told him that you are here, and he said, "That is bad!" I told him about Gloucester and that Edmund was a loyal friend. He said that I was a fool.'

'Our secret wishes will come true,' said Goneril to Edmund. 'This good servant will take my messages to you. Wear this jewel for me, Edmund. Let me kiss you.'

'Madam, my lord is coming,' whispered the servant, and Edmund went away.

'Oh, Goneril,' said Albany to his wife, 'you are an evil woman. You will come to a terrible end.'

'Do not say any more!' said Goneril. 'Your words are foolish.'

'Evil people believe that wise and good people are foolish. What have you done? You have made your father mad. Heaven will judge you.'

'Fool!' answered his wife. 'The King of France's army is here. Our country is not prepared. And you sit there and say, "Oh, why are they doing this?"'

At that moment a messenger rushed in.

'Do you have any news?' asked Albany.

'Oh, my lord, the Duke of Cornwall is dead. He went to take out Lord Gloucester's eyes and his servant wounded him. Now he is dead!'

'Oh, poor Gloucester! Has he lost both eyes?' said Albany.

'Both, both, my lord,' the messenger replied. Then he turned to Goneril. 'I have a letter from your sister, madam. You must answer it quickly.'

'Does Gloucester's son, Edmund, know what has happened?' asked Albany.

'Yes, my lord. Edmund told Cornwall that the Earl of Gloucester hoped for help from the French.'

Albany said, 'I must thank Gloucester. He has shown great love to the king. And I must punish those evil people who took out his eyes.'

◆

The French army was in a camp near Dover. Cordelia was with them, but the French king had returned to France because he was suddenly needed there.

Cordelia was speaking to her doctor in an army tent. 'Someone saw my father only a short time ago. He was as mad as the troubled sea waves. He was singing loudly and he was wearing a crown of flowers.'

She turned to an officer and said, 'Send out soldiers. Search every field and bring my father to me.' Then she asked the doctor, 'Is it possible to make his mind well again?'

'He needs to rest,' said the doctor. 'But there are also plants which will help him to forget his pain.'

'Search for him,' said Cordelia. 'I am afraid that he will try to kill himself.'

A messenger ran in. 'I have news, madam!' he cried. 'The British army is marching in this direction.'

'We know that already,' said Cordelia, 'and we are prepared. Oh, dear father, we have not come to take control of the country, but only to help you.'

◆

Goneril's servant came to Gloucester's castle, carrying a letter from Goneril to Edmund. Edmund was not in the castle, so Regan saw the letter.

'I do not like this,' said Regan. 'Why is she writing to Edmund? I am going to read this letter. Give it to me. I know that Goneril does not love her husband, and I have seen her look strangely at Edmund. Does she love him? Servant, you know everything that Goneril plans and thinks. Listen to me. My husband is dead. Edmund and I have talked. He is *my* man, not your lady's. Tell that to my sister.'

Then she said, 'And find that blind traitor Gloucester! I will give a lot to the person who kills him. People feel sorry for him, and that could harm us.'

◆

In the fields near Dover, Edgar was leading Gloucester by the hand.

'When will we come to the top of that high rock?' asked Gloucester.

'You are climbing up to it now,' answered Edgar. 'Isn't it hard work?'

'The ground feels flat to me.'

'No, it is very steep. Listen. Can you hear the sea?'

'No, I cannot,' Gloucester said.

'You have lost your eyes and your other senses are failing too. Come, sir. Here is the place. It is terrible to look down so far! The birds down there are the size of insects. The fishermen on the shore look like mice. I cannot look – I am afraid of falling!'

'Lead me to the place where you are standing,' ordered Gloucester.

'Give me your hand,' said Edgar. 'You are now just one step from the edge.'

'Leave my hand,' said Gloucester. 'Here is a purse, my friend. There is a valuable jewel inside it. You are a poor man – this jewel will make you rich. Go away, further away. Say goodbye to me. Let me hear you leave.'

'Goodbye, sir,' said Edgar.

'Now I must say goodbye to life,' said Gloucester. 'My sadness will end for ever. If Edgar is alive, God will take care of him.'

He stepped forward and fell – but he only fell on to the ground at his feet.

Now Edgar used a different voice to pretend to be somebody else.

'Alive or dead? Ah! You, sir, friend! Who are you, sir?'

'Go away!' said Gloucester. 'Go away and let me die!'

'It is wonderful that you are alive!' said Edgar. 'You must be a bird. You fell from such a terrible height and you did not break like an egg. Look up and see how far you fell.'

'I have no eyes. Am I still alive? I wanted to end my life.'

'Give me your arm,' Edgar said. 'Stand up. You can feel your legs. Who brought you to the top of the rock?'

'A poor unhappy beggar,' Gloucester replied.

'It was a devil, but the gods saved you.'

'Yes,' Gloucester said. 'From this moment, I will accept my troubles bravely. When my heart cries out, "Enough! Enough!" I will die.'

Lear came towards them, dressed in wild flowers.

'Oh!' cried Edgar. 'What a terrible sight!'

Lear came nearer, shouting mad words.

'I know that voice,' Gloucester said. 'It is the king. Let me kiss his hand.'

Then Cordelia's men arrived, looking for Lear.

'Here he is!' called their leader. 'Hold him! Your dear daughter has–'

'Daughter! Am I a prisoner?' cried Lear. 'Will nobody help me? I will die bravely! I am a king! Do you not know that?'

'You are the king, and we obey you,' the leader of the men said.

'Catch me, then! Run after me and catch me!' Lear ran away, and the others ran after him.

'Are you still there?' Gloucester asked Edgar. 'Who are you?'

'I am only a poor man,' Edgar answered. 'Take my hand, and I will lead you to a safe place.'

But Goneril's servant was there. 'Good,' he said. 'I have found Gloucester. His eyeless head will earn me a lot of money!'

He pulled out his sword, but Edgar stepped quickly between the man and Gloucester. He fought the servant without a sword, but he knocked the man down.

'Oh, I am going to die!' cried the servant. 'Take this bag. There is a letter inside it. Give the letter to Edmund and use the money to put me in a tomb.'

Edgar opened the letter. He read:

> *Remember our promises and kill my husband. Then I will be your wife.*
>
> *Goneril*

'I will show this letter to Albany,' Edgar said to himself. 'It is a good thing for him that I have learned his wife's plans.' Then he turned to Gloucester. 'Come, my lord,' he said, 'I will lead you to a friend who can help you and keep you safe. I can hear drums beating in the distance.'

◆

In a tent in the French camp, Cordelia was talking to the doctor.

'How is the king?' she asked.

'He is sleeping,' the doctor replied. 'I have dressed him in clean clothes and I will ask the servants to bring him here. Stay close to him when we wake him, my lady. I think he will get better.'

Cordelia kissed her father. 'This kiss will make you better. My two sisters have done great harm to you.'

She turned to the doctor. 'He is awake now,' she said. 'Speak to him.'

'It is better that you speak, madam.'

'Sir,' Cordelia said to her father, 'do you know me?'

'You have come from heaven,' Lear said. 'When did you die?'

'Oh, look at me, sir. Take my hand and give me your love. No! You must not fall to your knees!'

'I think I know you, but I am not sure,' Lear cried. 'Do not laugh at me. I think that this lady is my child, Cordelia.'

'She is! She is!' Cordelia wept.

'Do not weep! If you have poison for me, I will drink it. I know you cannot love me. Your sisters were bad to me. You have a reason to hate me, but they have not.'

'No, no! I do not hate you!'

'Am I in France?' Lear asked.

'You are in your own kingdom, sir,' Cordelia answered. 'Will you let me help you?'

'Yes, yes, dear daughter. Please forgive me. I am old and foolish.'

◆

Edmund was in the British camp near Dover. He was commander of the British army.

'Sweet lord,' said Regan to Edmund, 'tell me the truth. Do you love my sister Goneril? Are you close to her?'

'No, I promise you that I am not, madam,' Edmund replied.

Regan did not believe him. She thought it would be better to lose the coming battle than to lose this man to her sister.

Albany and Goneril arrived and they all prepared for battle. The sisters hated each other more than ever. Each sister knew that the other sister wanted Edmund.

In one of the tents, Albany spoke to Edgar, who was still pretending to be a stranger.

'Before you fight in battle,' said Edgar, 'open this letter. If you win, send for me. I can bring someone who will prove that the words in this letter are true.'

He went out, leaving Albany alone. Then Edmund came in. The enemy was very near, so Albany went to meet them with his army.

'I love both these sisters,' thought Edmund. 'Which shall I marry? If I choose Goneril, then Albany must die. He wants to forgive Lear and Cordelia, but I will not forgive them! If we win, they will fall into my power.'

◆

The battle was bitter. In the end, Edmund and the British army were more powerful than the French army. The British soldiers took Lear and Cordelia as prisoners.

'I am only worried about you,' Cordelia said to her father. 'I do not care about myself. Do you think we will see my sisters?'

'No!' said Lear. 'We must not see them! Let us go away to prison. When you ask for my love, I will ask you to forgive me. We will sing and tell old stories and laugh.'

'Take them away,' said Edmund. He sent for a captain. 'Your orders are in this letter. Will you obey me?'

'I will, sir,' the man said.

'Go, then, and do it. Do exactly what I say.'

Albany, Goneril, Regan and their soldiers arrived.

'You are holding the prisoners from this battle,' Albany said to Edmund. 'I want you to bring them here.'

'People feel very sorry for the old king,' Edmund said. 'I thought it was wise to keep him in a secret place. Soldiers are guarding him, and I sent Cordelia with him. I will bring them to you tomorrow.'

Albany was very angry that Edmund had taken Lear and Cordelia away without his permission. 'Sir,' he said to Edmund, 'in this war you are under my command.'

There was a quarrel. Edmund said that he was the new Earl of Gloucester. At the same time, the sisters quarrelled too. Each sister said that Edmund was her lover.

'You cannot say that you love him when you are married to me,' Albany said to Goneril. 'Edmund, you and Goneril are traitors. If no one else comes to prove it, I will prove it myself with my sword.'

Regan suddenly grew faint. 'Oh, I am ill!' she cried.

'If she is not ill,' thought Goneril, 'I have made a mistake and mixed her drink wrongly.'

'I will fight any man who calls me a traitor,' shouted Edmund.

'You will fight alone,' Albany replied. 'I have sent all your men away.'

'Oh! I feel worse!' said Regan. Albany ordered the servants to take her to her tent.

Then Edgar came in. He was carrying a sword, and his face was hidden.

'Pull out your sword,' he cried to Edmund. 'You were disloyal to your brother, your father and Lord Albany. You are a traitor!'

'My sword will answer you,' cried Edmund.

They fought and Edmund was wounded.

'This is a trick,' said Goneril. 'By the laws of war, you do not have to fight an enemy unless you know his name.'

'Shut your mouth, woman,' said Albany, 'or I will shut it with this paper.' He waved her letter to Edmund in the air. 'Ah! I can see that you recognize it!'

Goneril ran out.

'Who are you?' said Edmund to the man who had wounded him.

'My name is Edgar. I am your father's son.'

Albany took Edgar's hand. 'I never hated you or your father. Where did you hide? How did you know what happened to your father?'

In a few words Edgar told his story.

'Only half an hour ago,' he said, 'I told my father who I was. I told him everything. But, I am sorry to say, it was too much for his heart. His happiness and his sadness were too much for him, and he died.'

A man entered, holding a bloody knife in his hand.

'What does this mean?' asked Albany.

'Your lady, sir, your lady–'

'Lady Goneril poisoned Regan because of her love for me,' Edmund said. 'And now it seems that she has killed herself.'

Servants brought in the bodies of Goneril and Regan. Edmund was also dying.

'I am afraid of death,' he said. 'I must try to do one good act before I die. Send men to the castle. I told my soldiers to kill Lear and Cordelia. I gave them secret orders to make the people there say that Cordelia killed herself.'

After the servants carried Edmund away, Lear came in with Cordelia in his arms.

'I know when someone is dead and when she is alive,' he cried. She is as dead as the earth. A curse on you, you murderers. You are all traitors! I wanted to save her. Now she has gone for ever.'

He bent down and seemed to listen to her. 'Ha! Her voice was always soft, gentle and low. That is an excellent thing in a woman.'

A messenger came in. 'Edmund is dead, my lord.'

'And my poor child is dead,' said Lear. He could not breathe. 'Will you, please, undo this button . . . Thank you, sir.'

He fell, and Edgar ran to him. 'Look up, my lord. No – he is dead.'

'It is surprising that he lived for so long,' said Albany.

Edgar shook his head sadly. 'We younger ones must live with the unhappiness of these sad times.'

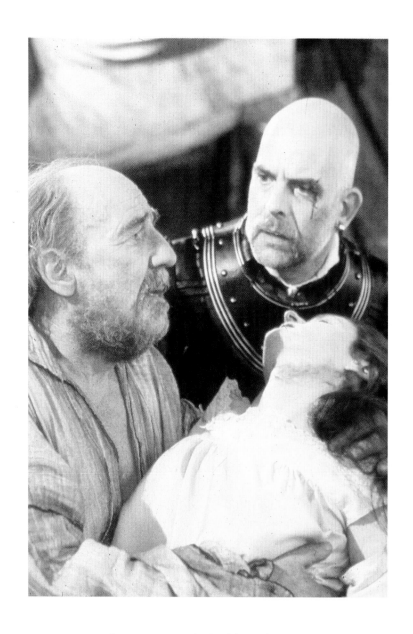

Lear came in with Cordelia in his arms.

ACTIVITIES

Romeo and Juliet

Before you read

1 This is a very famous love story. Have you seen it at the theatre, at the cinema or on television? What do you know about the story?

2 Find these words in your dictionary. They are all in the story.

cell Count dagger evil feast Friar hatred master sword tomb truth

  a Which words are titles or names for people?

  b Which are words for things that you fight with?

  c Which are words for places?

  d Which are bad qualities?

  e What is the opposite of a lie?

  f Which is a word for a big meal?

3 Find these verbs in your dictionary:

  beg curse quarrel weep wound

  a Which words are also nouns?

  b Which verb means:

    – cry?

    – hurt?

    – argue?

    – ask for money?

  What is the other verb in your language?

After you read

4 Answer these questions.

  a Why is Romeo unhappy at the beginning of the play? What happens when he meets Juliet?

  b Who is Friar Lawrence? How does he help Romeo and Juliet?

5 Describe the deaths of Romeo and Juliet in your own words.

6 List all the named characters who die in the story. How do they die?

7 Complete these sentences to show people's relationships with each other.

Juliet is Lord Capulet's .... Tybalt is Juliet's .... and Lord Capulet's .... The Prince of Verona is Paris's .... Paris wants to become Juliet's ....

Macbeth

Before you read

8 This is a play about Scotland in the eleventh century, when it was at war with England. Find Scotland on a map. What do you know about the relationship between the two countries now?

9 Answer questions about the words in *italics*. Use your dictionary to help you.

battle crown honour sorrow witch

a If there is a *battle* in an area, is the area peaceful?

b Who wears a *crown*? Where do they wear it?

c How can you *honour* a great writer?

d If your life is full of *sorrow*, how do you feel?

e Is a *witch* usually good or evil in stories?

After you read

10 Answer these questions.

a Why are the three witches important to the story?

b Why does Lady Macbeth wash her hands in her sleep?

c Why does Macbeth order Banquo's death?

d What is happening when Macbeth says, 'Do not shake your bloody hair at me!'?

e Why does Macbeth believe that nobody will kill him?

f How does 'Birnam Wood move to Dunsinane'?

11 Which named characters die in this story? How do they die?

12 Discuss the characters of Macbeth and Lady Macbeth. What are their good and bad qualities? Which of them do you think is most evil?

King Lear

Before you read

13 King Lear has three daughters. He decides to share his kingdom between them because he is too old to govern. What do you think will happen next?

14 Find these words in your dictionary. Make sentences with them.

    a *trust   devil*

    b *duke   traitor*

    c *bastard   earl*

    d *knight   plot   kingdom*

After you read

15 What are the relationships between these people?

King Lear is Regan, Goneril and Cordelia's .... The Duke of Albany is Goneril's .... Regan is married to the .... Edmund is Edgar's .... The Earl of Gloucester is their ....

16 Discuss how these characters die. Do they deserve to die? Why (not)?

    a Regan

    b Goneril

    c Edmund

    d Cordelia

17 Work with other students. Choose a scene from the story and act it out. Explain why you chose that scene.

Writing

18 You are making a film of *Romeo and Juliet*. You must advise the actress who is playing Juliet. What do you want her to do when she wakes up in the tomb? Write down your advice. Start like this: *When you wake up, and before you look round, smile happily. . .*

19 Imagine that you are Lady Macbeth. Write a page in your diary describing the murder of Duncan and what happens afterwards.

20 Compare the three sisters in *King Lear*. What are their characters like? How do they behave towards their father?

21 Choose a main character from one of the stories. Write the story from their experience of it.

22 Which of the plays would you like to see at the theatre? Explain why.

23 Shakespeare wrote these plays nearly 400 years ago. Why do you think they are still so popular?

Answers for the Activities in this book are available from your local office or alternatively write to: Penguin Readers Marketing Department, Pearson Education, Edinburgh Gate, Harlow, Essex CM20 2JE.